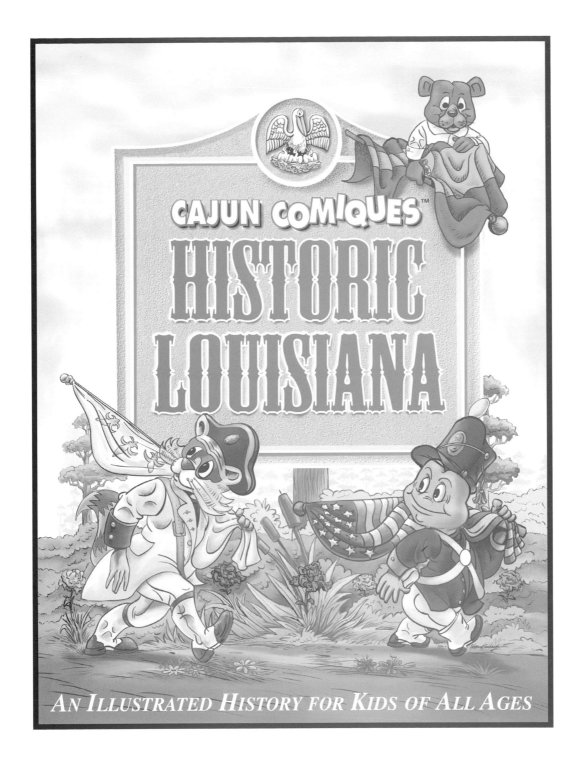

CAJUN COMIQUES™
HISTORIC LOUISIANA

AN ILLUSTRATED HISTORY FOR KIDS OF ALL AGES

Written by
Guy N. Faucheux & Wallace P. Faucheux

Illustrated by
Wallace P. Faucheux

st. roux press

Mandeville, Louisiana

Guy N Faucheux
NOV 8, 2003

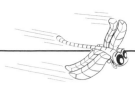

CAJUN COMIQUES HISTORIC LOUISIANA
An Illustrated History for Kids of All Ages

ISBN 0-9718433-1-7

Written by Guy N. Faucheux and Wallace P. Faucheux

Illustrated by Wallace P. Faucheux

Production Coordination by Aimée F. Faucheux

Editing by Deanne R. Faucheux, Jeanne H. Faucheux,
David Schultz, and Eugenie Miltenberger Martin

Published by St. Roux Press
Exclusive Publishers of Cajun Comiques
P. O. Box 1815
Mandeville, LA 70470

Phone: 985-796-3946
Fax: 985-796-1815
Email: strouxpress@i-55.com
www.cajuncomiques.com

First Edition

Copyright © 2003 by Guy N. Faucheux and Wallace P. Faucheux

The Cajun Comiques, the Cajun Comiques Characters,
the Gumbeaux Kids, and the Les Petits Comiques are trademarks
of Guy N. Faucheux and Wallace P. Faucheux

Printed in Taiwan

Publisher's Cataloging-in-Publication Data

Faucheux, Guy N.
    Cajun Comiques historic Louisiana : an illustrated
history for kids of all ages / written by Guy N.
Faucheux & Wallace P. Faucheux ; illustrated by Wallace
P. Faucheux -- 1st ed.
    p. cm.
    Includes bibliographical references and index.
    SUMMARY: The Cajun Comiques, a fun loving but hard
working family of cartoon characters, communicate the
joie de vivre of Louisiana history to young readers.
    Audience: Grade 6-8.
    ISBN 0-9718433-1-7

    1. Louisiana--History--Juvenile literature.
    [1. Louisiana--History.]   I. Faucheux, Wallace. II. Title.

F369.3.F38 2003   976.3
                            QBI33-795

Foreword

Before beginning their tale, the authors of *CAJUN COMIQUES HISTORIC LOUISIANA — An Illustrated History for Kids of All Ages* want to provide a little background about their storytelling approach. As storytellers their goal for this publication is to communicate accurately the early history of Louisiana while at the same time offering, through entertaining illustrations, a taste of the region's well-known multicultural charm.

The period of Louisiana history covered in this book, 1682–1815, is very complex, considering that the text spans the cultural history of French Colonists, Acadians, Spanish Creoles, Native Americans, West Africans, *decima*-singing Isleños, Germans from the *Côte des Allemands*, Italians, Scots, Irish, and other peoples of unique origins who settled throughout the state of Louisiana. Thus, to ensure historical accuracy, the authors consulted numerous research sources, which are referenced in the Bibliography.

To add a little spice to the storytelling, phrases of Cajun French are sprinkled in here and there. As the Cajun language has been traditionally oral, not written, an authoritative source was needed. Their source for written Cajun is *A Dictionary of the Cajun Language* by Rev. Msgr. Jules O. Daigle. The dictionary's First Limited Edition is always on the top of their stack of reference materials.

The charm of the *Cajun Comiques* results from a collaborative effort between the authors — one a graphic artist and both Louisiana history enthusiasts. The authors grew up in Louisiana surrounded by the unique Cajun language and culture. Both experienced first hand the *joie de vivre* associated with Louisiana's outdoor life, fabulous cuisine, vibrant music, and close family ties. Through the *Cajun Comiques*, whom you will meet in the following pages, the authors hope to fully share with kids of all ages the history, flavor, and fun of Louisiana's storied past.

Meet The Cajun Comiques™

The *Cajun Comiques* are a fun-loving yet hard-working family of cartoon characters who share a common calling for communicating with others the *joie de vivre* — joy of life — associated with historic Louisiana. Each character represents, in part, one ingredient in the fascinating multicultural gumbo created by French Colonialists, Acadians, Spanish Creoles, Native Americans, West Africans, *decima*-singing Isleños, Germans from the *Côte des Allemands*, Italians, Scots, Irish, and other people of unique origins whose descendants now call Louisiana home.

François Ferret™

Toulouse Le Turtle™

Etienne Chien™

Mademoiselle Minou™

Prosper Le Pélican™

Nenaine Nutria™

Prudent 'Possum™

Yvest Egret™

Parrain 'Possum™

Roger Raccoon™

Guidaux Gator™

Mémere Muskrat™

Jacques Lapin™

Beauregard Bullfrog™

Antoine Hebert™

The *Cajun Comiques* inhabit the fascinating wetlands, coastal marshes, and prairies of the Cajun Country parishes, as well as the Plantation Country along the Mississippi and Louisiana's Crossroads that run through the city of Alexandria. You will also find them in Natchitoches and the Red River, the Sportsman's Paradise of Louisiana's Northern Parishes, and the Greater New Orleans area. The Comiques' mission is to promote the heritage and values of Louisiana as a whole so that they and *les enfants* of Bayou Country, the *Gumbeaux Kids*™, might share with readers of all ages the warmth and richness of the home they affectionately refer to as *Historic Louisiana*.

Historic Louisiana
Table of Contents

Meet Les Petits Comiques™

Throughout the pages of this book, the *Cajun Comiques* will be assisted by their little friends — *Les Petits Comiques*. When additional insight in regard to language, historical facts, or fun activities is needed, these little guys will be there to help.

Welcome
to Historic
Louisiana

1

Somewhere deep in Bayou Country . . .

On their way home from their first day back at school, the Gumbeaux Kids are eager to stop at N'Oncle Yvest's General Store   They can't wait to tell him all about their day.

Jay Peep   *René Raccoon*   *Ti Bear*   *Aimée Muskrat*

As *les enfants*, or the little ones of Bayou Country, these special *Cajun Comiques* will add their own insight to our tale of *Historic Louisiana*. So look for Jay Peep, René, Ti Bear, and Aimée along the way as they give their own unique perspective to our story.

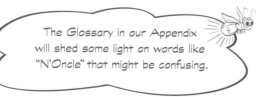

The Glossary in our Appendix will shed some light on words like "N'Oncle" that might be confusing.

Let the Story begin . . .

N'ONCLE YVEST: *Bonjour, mes enfants!* How was your first day back at school?

GUMBEAUX KIDS: N'Oncle Yvest, our teacher Mademoiselle Minou gave us too much homework! She already assigned us a class project. The project is about our heritage. We come from the bayou — how can we do a project like that?

N'ONCLE YVEST: *Mais, ecoute dont ça!* You know, when you come from Louisiana, there are millions of things to discover about your heritage!

N'ONCLE YVEST: Our heritage is like a tasty gumbo. A gumbo, as you know, is made from many rich ingredients added to a roux, which we then slowly cook together for a long time.

GUMBEAUX KIDS: That sounds like Louisiana! Do you mean G-U-M-B-O, or is that G-U-M-B-E-A-U-X?

N'ONCLE YVEST: Yes, you kids are very quick! We are talking about a type of gumbo very different from the one we cook at home. Ours is a unique multicultural gumbo. So, let me explain . . . I inherited these early Louisiana gumbo recipes from my great grandpère, Emile Egret. They were given to him by his great grandpère, one of the first settlers in historic Louisiana. Legend has it that he was with Bienville when he became Louisiana's first governor. Like these recipes, Louisiana has quite a history!

GUMBEAUX KIDS: N'Oncle Yvest, who was Bee-yen-vill?

N'ONCLE YVEST: Oooh weee! You've never heard of Bienville? *Mes chères*! We have some work to do. Gather 'round and listen closely, and I will tell you what great grandpère Emile passed on to me when he gave me these recipes so long ago. Now, before we get to Bienville, we must first go all the way back to when the French first discovered and settled Louisiana.

French
Discovery
and
Settlement

N'ONCLE YVEST,
DID THE FRENCH REALLY
DISCOVER LOUISIANA?

MES CHÈRES,
LET ME TELL YOU
ALL ABOUT IT . . .

By the late seventeenth century, major European powers were in fierce competition to expand their borders the fastest and the farthest. At that time, three nations battled for control of the New World — Spain, France, and England — each seeking land and treasure!

Spain, as far back as the 1500s, had obtained vast fortunes of gold in Mexico, Central and South America . . .

France, by the mid-1600s, had created New France in Canada . . .

. . . and England was settling its American colonies on the Atlantic coast.

Thus, the seventeenth century found the map of the North American continent divided among the major colonizing forces of Spain, France, and England. France controlled the upper reach of North America, which would one day become Canada. England was busy with its American colonies while the Spanish possessed the majority of the South, controlling Mexico, Florida, and Cuba. This left vast unclaimed territory in the continent's interior to be discovered and settled.

In the Americas, Spain acquired gold and silver; England created wealth from working the land, and the French prospered from the fur trade. Each, however, was always in search of just a little bit more!

In the year 1682, the French Canadian explorer Robert de La Salle and his companion Henri di Tonti traveled south from Montreal, Canada into the unclaimed territory of North America, seeking once again to expand France's holdings.

After months of grueling effort, the Canadians made it all the way down the Illinois River to the Mississippi — *The Father of Waters.*

At the mouth of the river, where it flows into the Gulf of Mexico, La Salle laid claim to the entire Mississippi Valley as part of New France.

As a result, all lands east to the Appalachian Mountains and west to the Rocky Mountains were considered part of New France. The explorers named the region *La Louisiane* after King Louis XIV (14th), who is known to history as the *Sun King.*

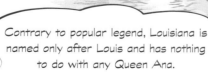

Contrary to popular legend, Louisiana is named only after Louis and has nothing to do with any Queen Ana.

Two years later, in 1684, La Salle led an expedition from France to establish a colony in *La Louisiane*, the territory he had claimed for King Louis XIV. Unfortunately, the travelers made a navigational error in the Gulf of Mexico, and the expedition, which landed on the Texas coast, ended in disaster. As a result, French colonization plans in the region were put on hold.

A few years after La Salle's misfortune, in 1698, France renewed its interest in *La Louisiane*, and Louis, Comte de Pontchartrain, the King's Minister of Marine, drew up plans for colonizing the Mississippi Valley. La Salle's efforts would not be in vain after all as France's claim would now be backed up by military action!

At the court in Versailles, palace of Louis XIV, Pontchartrain gave orders to a naval officer from Montreal, Canada — Pierre le Moyne, Sieur d'Iberville. Iberville's orders were to establish an additional fort in the territory claimed by La Salle. Pontchartrain felt that this fort, with others in Canada and the Illinois territory, was needed to protect France's territorial claim to *La Louisiane*.

Born in Canada, which was then New France, Iberville understood the French concept of a colony. As a colony, *La Louisiane* would be treated like any other French province. *La Louisiane* would have the same laws, same customs, and same religion as France. The King's soldiers would be organized as in every other French colony. So, whether the men in Iberville's expedition were from Normandy in France or Quebec in Canada, they would each come to *La Louisiane* as soldiers of the King.

In 1698, when Iberville set sail from Brest, France, it was with a crew of both French and Canadian sailors. Months later in January 1699, they sailed into the Gulf of Mexico and, anticipating they were near the mouth of La Salle's Mississippi, constructed a temporary fort at present day Biloxi, Mississippi. From there, Iberville, his crew, and many of the soldiers they transported entered the Mississippi and explored the river and surrounding waterways.

LAKE MAUREPAS

LAKE PONTCHARTRAIN
← 42 miles →

LAKE BORGNE

BATON ROUGE
← 80 miles from Nouvelle Orleans

BILOXI 93 miles →

MOBILE 141 miles from Nouvelle Orleans →

MISSISSIPPI RIVER

NOUVELLE ORLEANS

Lake Borgne wasn't named after a person. *Borgne* means *one-eyed* — as the lake is only half a lake, as French sailors saw it.

Quelle bonheur!
What luck!

While exploring the river, the expedition met a Bayougoula tribesman who possessed a letter written by Tonti seventeen years earlier. The letter was good news. It confirmed that they had indeed found La Salle's Mississippi! Along the Mississippi, Iberville and his crew also observed red poles on the river's banks. The poles, called *Istrouma* by the local Native Americans, marked their tribal boundaries. Iberville named the Istrouma site *Baton Rouge*, which is French for *Red Stick*.

While exploring, Iberville also named lakes after Pontchartrain and his son, Comte de Maurepas. Sometime after these discoveries, Iberville was ordered away to war, leaving his younger brother Jean Baptiste le Moyne, Sieur de Bienville in charge of the more permanent fort at present day Mobile, Alabama. Protecting the colony from military threats and raging hurricanes was now the young eighteen-year-old Bienville's responsibility.

In 1706, Bienville received the sad news that his brother Iberville had died in Cuba. With Iberville's passing, Bienville knew his brother would have wanted a more secure location for the colony. So he sailed from Mobile to Lake Borgne and through the Rigolets into Lake Pontchartrain in search of a new site for the colony. After scouting the entire region, Bienville sailed up Bayou St. Jean and followed an Indian path to the Mississippi River. He selected high ground on a crescent bend of the river. There the French could defend themselves, using the timber of this cypress wilderness to build a stockade. In 1718, work began on the site they nicknamed *Cité Croissant* — the *Crescent City*. Officially, Bienville named it *Nouvelle Orleans* — New Orleans. The name was in honor of the Louis XIV's only brother — *Duc d'Orleans* — the Duke of Orleans.

N'ONCLE YVEST WOULD SAY THAT BIENVILLE PUT THE COLONY TOGETHER LIKE A GOOD GUMBO. AND LIKE ANY GUMBO, BIENVILLE STARTED WITH A ROUX.

OH, I SEE NOW WHAT MADEMOISELLE MINOU'S PROJECT IS GETTING AT! *La Louisiane's* ROUX IS ITS RICH SOIL — THICK AND DARK.

... AND UPON THIS DARK EARTHY ROUX BIENVILLE BUILT THE COLONY.

SO, FOR BIENVILLE, BUILDING THE COLONY WAS LIKE COOKING UP A UNIQUE CULTURAL GUMBO — WHAT WE KIDS WOULD CALL "GUMBEAUX."

MISSISSIPPI RIVER

You see, *mes chères*, the city of *Nouvelle Orleans* was laid out by Bienville's engineers as a *carré*. Carré is a French word meaning a square or rectangle. Building what is known today as the Vieux Carré required the engineers to survey the land and mark its boundaries. They drained swamp water from the site, removed countless cypress trees, and turned the grids of the engineers' plans into actual streets.

For a fun day trip from the French Quarter, check out the National Park Service Barataria Preserve in Marrero. See what the swamps around New Orleans must have looked like to Bienville and his military engineers.

MANY CITY STREETS IN *Nouvelle Orleans* — RUE BURGUNDY, BOURBON, CHARTRES, CONTI, AND TOULOUSE — WERE GIVEN THE FAMILY NAMES OF FRENCH NOBILITY DURING THE ADMINISTRATION OF THE *Duc d'Orleans* WHO, AFTER THE DEATH OF HIS BROTHER KING LOUIS XIV, ACTED AS REGENT FOR THE VERY YOUNG FRENCH KING — LOUIS XV.

All around the Vieux Carré, Bienville's soldiers were put to work building fortified walls from the felled cypress trees. Meanwhile, in the center of *Nouvelle Orleans*, his engineers selected a site for a church. The church would be Catholic — the state religion of France and its colonies. The French named the church in honor of St. Louis, Patron Saint of France and King Louis XIV's namesake.

Saint Louis was also France's Crusader King, Louis the IX, not King Louis the XIV. The Sun King was certainly no saint.

In the front of the church, where Jackson Square is now situated, stood the *Place d'Armes* — a drill field for the fort's French soldiers. There the soldiers trained before being sent to one of a number of military outposts in the colony such as Baton Rouge, Rapides (near Alexandria), Pointe Coupee, Natchitoches, Ouachita (Monroe), Opelousas, Attakapas (St. Martinville), Arkansas, Illinois, and many others. These military outposts also became colonial settlements. The historic town of Natchitoches, for instance, was among the earliest, founded in 1715 by the French Canadian officer Louis de Saint-Denis.

In *La Louisiane*, both European French and Canadian French soldiers served as members of small military companies — the *compagnies détachées*. It was a tough assignment for any soldier. Military discipline, the heat, disease, along with inadequate pay, supplies, food, and uniforms, much less the loneliness of isolated outposts, made the colony a hard place to serve the king.

After completing military service in *La Louisiane*, many members of these French military companies never went home. Instead, Bienville, who was now Governor, allowed his soldiers to retire from their service to the King, settle in the colony, and become part of the civilian population. Many of the European French soldiers may have preferred to settle close to civilization, but the Canadian French, known as the *coureur de bois*, tended to favor the wide open spaces the wilderness of *La Louisiane* provided.

INSIDE THIS CAULDRON, EARLY SETTLERS AND RETIRED "COMPAGNIES DÉTACHÉES" WOULD MIX TOGETHER OVER TIME.

NATIVE AMERICAN WAYS, LIKE SAVORY INGREDIENTS ADDED TO A ROUX, BLENDED WITH THE FRENCH TRADITIONS TO BECOME PART OF THE CULTURAL GUMBO *La Louisiane* IS FAMOUS FOR.

CHOCTAW FILÉ — NOW THAT'S GOOD STUFF!

Nouvelle Orleans WAS LIKE A BIG CAULDRON FOR THE COLONY'S CULTURAL GUMBO.

Looking out from Yvest Egret's store, the region's landscape reminds us that the multi-cultural gumbo of *La Louisiane* comes from more than just French stock. Native Americans, with their ancient knowledge of the land and waters, greatly assisted Bienville's colonists. Members of many different tribes taught the settlers how to capture the region's now famous seafood — fish, oysters, crabs, and shrimp. The Native Americans also taught the settlers how to prepare *filé* for gumbo from the native sassafras tree, to pick wild blackberries, to catch crawfish in the swamps, and even to make canoe-like pirogues for navigating the wetlands of *La Louisiane*.

Today, there are four sovereign Indian tribes of Louisiana that include the Chitamacha, Tunica-Biloxi, Coushatta, and the Jena Band of Choctaw. From the languages of these and other tribes, the coureur de bois adopted names for the region's many waterways. Mississippi, Atchafalaya, and Tchefuncte are all of Native American origin as are the names of the cities of Houma, Opelousas, and Ponchatoula. The civil parishes of Plaquemines, Avoyelles, Natchitoches, Caddo, and Tangipahoa and even some city street names, such as New Orleans' Tchoupitoulas (Chop-a-TOO-less), are also of Native American origin.

As terrible as we know it to be today, many people then thought slavery was necessary for colonial success. Starting in 1719 when the first slave ships arrived in *La Louisiane* from Senegal, the strength of West Africans was used to establish indigo and sugar industries in the colony. Through their skills, they transformed places such as *Nouvelle Orleans* from a swampy, mosquito-infested wilderness into the Vieux Carré we see today.

Though enslaved, West Africans significantly impacted *La Louisiane* through their craftsmanship and traditions, contributing greatly in many ways to its multicultural heritage. Much of the distinctive cooking of *La Louisiane* really originated in their colonial kitchens. In addition, the musical sounds known today as jazz, along with rhythm and blues, are said to have grown out of slave gatherings in places such as Congo Square (known today as Armstrong Park) right outside the Vieux Carré. And in Southwest *La Louisiane*, French-speaking West Africans developed the musical tradition we know today as zydeco.

With sites such as the Jazz Museum at the Old U. S. Mint in the Vieux Carré, the New Orleans African-American Museum, and the African-American Museum in St. Martinville, Louisiana has made a significant effort to recognize the region's West African ties. Be sure to stop in and learn more about this part of Louisiana's unique multicultural heritage.

HEY, EVERYBODY SHOULD KNOW THAT *Gumbo* IS WEST AFRICAN FOR *Okra* AND THAT IT WAS INTRODUCED INTO THE COLONY BY WEST AFRICANS.

THOUGH AFRICANS WERE BROUGHT TO *La Louisiane* AGAINST THEIR WILL, THEY ARE SOME OF THE MOST SIGNIFICANT CONTRIBUTORS TO THE REGION'S CULTURAL GUMBO!

FOR THAT MATTER, RED BEANS AND RICE WERE TOO.

AND DON'T FORGET THE JAZZ, MAN!

In early colonial days, *La Louisiane* had soldiers, laborers, musicians, and very good cooks — but few farmers. The colony desperately needed skilled farmers capable of cultivating the land. How can one make Okra Gumbo or Red Beans and Rice without vegetables? But convincing productive farmers to settle in Louisiana was a difficult task. Somehow, John Law, a clever Scottish promoter and land speculator, found a way.

Surprisingly, the hardy farmers he convinced were not French, but German. As a result, starting in 1719, many Germans crossed the Atlantic and eventually settled upriver from *Nouvelle Orleans*. These early German settlers were known to the French in *La Louisiane* as *les Allemands,* and their habitation — *Côte des Allemands*. There today you will find in Louisiana's German Coast the town of Des Allemands, along with the waterways of Lac des Allemands and Bayou des Allemands.

LES ALLEMANDS QUICKLY ADOPTED THE FRENCH LANGUAGE OF THE COLONY. IN THE LOUISIANA COUNTRYSIDE YOU WILL NOT FIND ANY "SAUERKRAUT" OR "SCHNITZEL."

YOU WILL FIND MANY GERMAN FAMILY NAMES, HOWEVER, SUCH AS HYMEL, WAGUESPACK, VICKNAIR, SCHEXNAYDRE, TROXCLAIR, ZERINGUE AND MANY OTHERS. THE ANCESTORS OF THESE FAMILIES ALL CAME TO *La Louisiane* IN THOSE EARLY COLONIAL YEARS.

LES ALLEMANDS SUPPLIED THE STAPLES OF THE REGIONAL CUISINE — TOMATOES, PEPPERS, OKRA, ONIONS, SUGAR, AND GARLIC.

OVER TIME, THESE HARD WORKING ALLEMANDS BECAME AN INFLUENTIAL INGREDIENT IN THE COLONY'S GUMBEAUX.

For years, the hard-working Germans had lived peacefully in French-ruled *La Louisiane* under the leadership of Governor Bienville. About the time of his departure in 1743, life for the Germans' future neighbors, living way to the north, began to change for the worse. With the Treaty of Utrecht in 1713, French holdings in parts of Canada including all of *Acadia* had been turned over to the British. In 1755, after years of contentious refusals to swear allegiance to the British Crown, French settlers in what the British named Nova Scotia were deported. The Acadians were expelled to such places as New York, Philadelphia, Baltimore, and beyond. In time, many of these exiled Acadians would make their way to *La Louisiane*, becoming the first wave of the colony's most famous settlers.

Both the established Germans and the newly arriving Acadians were jolted in 1766 when they learned France had ceded *La Louisiane* to the Spanish, thus making it Spain's colony of *La Luisiane*. French military outposts throughout the colony would now be manned by Spanish soldiers. French street names in the Vieux Carré were changed to reflect the new Spanish rule. *Rue Royale* became *Calle Real*. And the seat of government was located in the *Cabildo* — a building distinctively Spanish in architecture. But we are getting ahead of ourselves. Let's first see how Spain came to acquire France's *La Louisiane . . .*

Spain Takes Colonial Control

Spain acquires La Louisiane . . .

While the French were settling the newly arriving Acadians in the wilderness of *La Louisiane*, a war was raging in other parts of New France. France was fighting the English along with their respective Native American allies in what we know in America as the French and Indian War. It was a winner-take-all struggle with each side seeking total control of North America.

IN EUROPE, IT WAS CALLED THE "SEVEN YEARS WAR."

FIGHTING AND COOKING DON'T MIX.

CAN WE GET BACK TO COOKING?

FRENCH AND INDIAN WAR! THAT'S WHAT THE BRITISH CALLED IT.

During the French and Indian War, America's own George Washington first proved himself as a military leader, fighting with the English against the French. Most of the fighting during the French and Indian War took place far north of *La Louisiane* in French-speaking Canada and the English-speaking colonies of North America.

The British, with the help of Washington and the colonial militia in the English colonies, eventually defeated France in 1763. This defeat at the hand of Great Britain resulted in a significant loss of influence and wealth for France as their domination in North America was forcibly brought to an end!

French concessions to the British were outlined in the 1763 Treaty of Paris. The treaty spelled out the terms of the French surrender and required the government in France to turn over most of its North American holdings to England. Those holdings, as the British figured it, included all of Canada, lands east of the Mississippi all the way to the Appalachian Mountains, lands west of the Mississippi, and the *Isle d'Orleans*. At that time, the *Isle d'Orleans* referred to lands on the east bank of the Mississippi River south of Baton Rouge down to the mouth of the river.

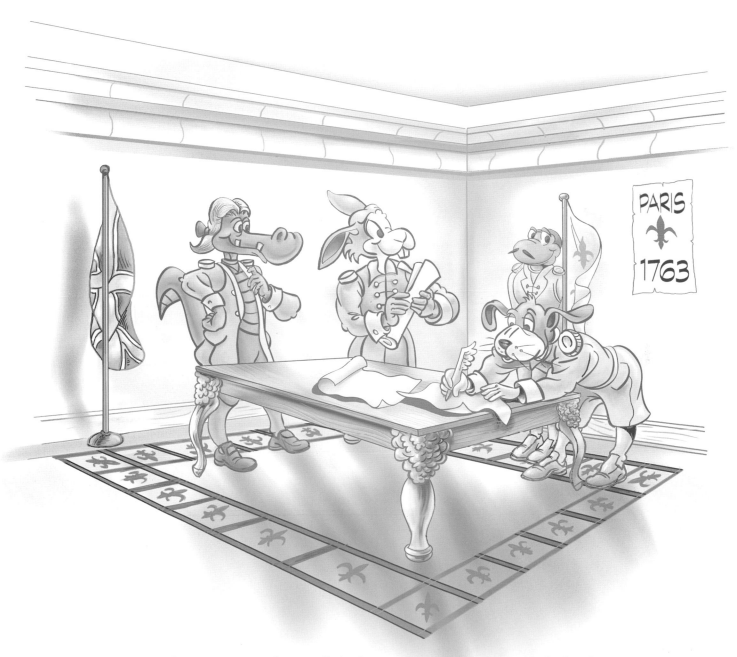

After the Treaty of Paris, most of La Salle's claim east of the Mississippi, the St. Lawrence River Valley, Quebec, and Montreal passed from French to British control. In addition, because Spain aided France late in the war, Spain also was forced to cede its entire Florida territory to the victorious English. But the lands west of the Mississippi and the *Isle d'Orleans*, as we shall see, did not pass into British hands.

In 1762, after the English victory but before the 1763 Treaty of Paris was signed, an interesting twist to the history of *La Louisiane* occurred. Just months before the treaty was signed, King Louis XV of France ceded some of the colony to his cousin — King Carlos III of Spain.

At the palace at Fountainbleu, the French handoff to Spain assured that England would not take control of *La Louisiane's* western territory or the *Isle d'Orleans*. As might be expected, *La Louisiane's* French colonists at first were not happy with their new Spanish rulers — in fact, they rebelled. Thus, in 1769 King Carlos would require the firm hand of the Irish-born military governor General Alejandro O'Reilly to make the French-speaking colonists see things the Spanish way. So, through a series of very surprising events, the Spanish lost Florida but found themselves rulers of French-speaking *La Louisiane* for a time.

It was while Spain ruled *La Louisiane* that the American Revolution began. As everyone knows, at that time George Washington was fighting against the British, not for them. In fact, Washington was leading the American War of Independence. And on the eastern seaboard the American war effort, interestingly enough, was being aided by the French through the leadership of a remarkable young military officer — the Marquis de Lafayette.

Meanwhile on the Gulf Coast, the Spanish also began aiding the American war effort. In 1776, the Spanish government in *Nouvelle Orleans* gave Washington's army needed supplies, thus enabling the Americans to push the British out of the Ohio Valley and back into Canada. Starting in 1779, *La Louisiane's* French Acadian and German militiamen joined by the colony's West Africans fought with the Spanish during the American Revolution. Under the leadership of the energetic Spanish Governor Bernardo de Gálvez, the colony's militia forced the British to surrender forts they had occupied at Manchac, Baton Rouge, Natchez, Mobile, and Pensacola, thereby pushing the British out of Florida, which greatly assisted the American cause.

The first wave of Acadian immigration to *La Louisiane* started soon after their expulsion from Nova Scotia in 1755. When the Spanish finally took control of the colony in 1769, this first wave was coming to an end. The immigrants settled on the banks of the Mississippi above the Côte des Allemands in what became known as the First Acadian Coast. They also settled on the prairies of Southwest *La Louisiane* near Postes des Opelousas and Attakapas (present day St. Martinville). These prairie settlements were reached via scenic waterways such as Bayou Teche — the only highways *La Louisiane* possessed. Although colonization slowed during the conflict with England, after the American Revolution, the Spanish accelerated settlement of *La Louisiane's* wide open wilderness.

Settling *La Louisiane* with its rivers, bayous, prairies, swamps, and salt marsh wetlands required a bold vision. The Spanish Governor's vision for the colony included the subsequent settlement of the Second Acadian Coast and Bayou Lafourche. The Governor also sought Spanish settlers to overcome the immense obstacles *La Louisiane's* wilderness presented. Between 1778 and 1782, more than 2,000 settlers from the Spanish mainland and the Canary Islands were recruited as colonists. These Spaniards would join the prospering German and Acadian settlers to wrestle a living from the land and waters of *La Louisiane*.

Under the leadership of the Spanish military officer Francisco Bouligny, colonists from the Spanish town of Málaga settled on Bayou Teche and established the settlement of *Nuevo Iberia* — what is today New Iberia.

The Canary Islanders, or *Isleños*, as they were known in Spanish, settled in different parts of the colony. One of their major settlements was deep in the wetlands of the colony, down the Mississippi from *Nouvelle Orleans*. In what was known as *Terre-aux-Boeufs*, present day St. Bernard Parish, these colonists settled in to live a hearty outdoor life as trappers and fishermen. And from their islands off the Spanish coast, they brought the *decima* for entertainment. The decima is a Spanish ballad, a form of musical poetry that tells a story. Over the years, the Isleños kept their unique culture alive in *La Louisiane* through the telling of stories in song.

THE ISLEÑOS ALSO BROUGHT THEIR FLAVORFUL CULTURE TO THE COLONY, MAKING *La Louisiane's* GUMBEAUX MUCH MORE SAVORY!

WHERE CAN YOU STILL HEAR THE "ISLEÑO" DECIMA SOUNDS TODAY?

JUST CHECK WITH THE "LOS ISLEÑOS HERITAGE AND CULTURAL SOCIETY" IN ST. BERNARD PARISH.

THE ISLEÑOS INTRODUCED SPANISH NAMES INTO THE COLONY SUCH AS DIAZ, PEREZ, NUNEZ, FERNANDEZ, RODRIGUEZ, HERNANDEZ, RUIZ, AND MANY OTHERS NOT ENDING IN "Z".

Following the Isleños, the new Spanish Governor Don Esteban Miró welcomed a second wave of French-speaking Acadian settlers. They arrived in 1785 in seven ships chartered by Spain to bring the colonists to *La Louisiane*. The lead ship was named *Bon Papa*. Much earlier when the Acadians had been deported from *Acadia*, their Canadian paradise, many had been shipped back to France where they were stranded for many years. Eventually, 1,500 Acadians found passage to *La Louisiane* in order to join friends and family who had settled in the colony more than twenty years earlier.

THIS IS SO SAD!

Tres Malheureux. THE SITUATION TURNED OUT REALLY BAD FOR THE ACADIANS IN WHAT IS NOW KNOWN AS NOVA SCOTIA.

THE ACADIANS' TROUBLES STARTED WITH POLITICAL EVENTS FOLLOWING THE BRITISH TAKEOVER OF ACADIA.

AS BAD AS IT WAS FOR THEM THERE, HERE IN *La Louisiane*, THEY LEARNED TO MAKE A REALLY GOOD GUMBO.

Friendless, homeless, hopeless,
they wandered from city to city,

From the cold lakes of the North
to sultry Southern savannas.

Friends they sought and homes;
and many, despairing, heart-broken,

Asked of the earth but a grave, and
no longer a friend nor a fireside.

from *Evangeline*
by Henry Wadsworth Longfellow

In 1847, the American poet Henry Wadsworth Longfellow memorialized the hardship of the French-speaking Acadians in his narrative poem *Evangeline, A Tale of Acadie.* The poem tells the story of two young lovers separated during the Acadian's *Grand Derangement.* The words of *Evangeline,* her statue in St. Martinville, and the weeping moss on Louisiana's oaks, all reflect the sad lament of the Acadian experience.

TODAY, THE LONG GRAY GROWTH ON LOUISIANA'S OAKS IS CALLED "SPANISH MOSS."

THE COLONIAL SPANISH CALLED THE MOSS "FRENCH WIGS."

BUT THE FRENCH CALLED THE MOSS "SPANISH BEARDS."

EVANGELINE — SHE IS JUST SO DREAMY!

After surviving their tribulation, the second wave of Acadians must have felt doubly blessed when, in 1785, Spanish Governor Miró issued them land grants on the Second Acadian Coast along Bayou Lafourche and on additional sites in the Southwest Prairies of *La Louisiane*. They happily joined previously settled family members in *La Nouvelle Acadie* who, by 1768, had established themselves in the First Acadian Coast and the Postes des Opelousas and Attakapas.

With their ability to farm, fish, hunt, and trap, the Acadians became productive colonists for Spain. Their descendants in and around Thibodaux, Houma, Jeanerette, Lafayette, Breaux Bridge, Abbeville, Eunice, Opelousas, St. Martinville, Marksville, Ville Platte, Crowley, Jennings, Welsh, Lake Charles, and many other towns produced the unique culture of Acadian Louisiana whose savory food and vibrant music we know so well today as Cajun.

LEARN MORE ABOUT THEM AT THE RURAL LIFE MUSEUM IN BATON ROUGE.

OR CHECK OUT ACADIAN VILLAGE AND VERMILIONVILLE IN LAFAYETTE.

THE INFLUENCE OF THE "CAJUNS" IS CONSIDERED THE MAIN INGREDIENT OF THE REGION'S CULTURAL GUMBO.

THE LONGFELLOW-EVANGELINE HISTORIC SITE IS ALSO A MUST SEE.

During Spanish rule, as new settlers like the Acadians and Isleños moved to the countryside, *Nouvelle Orleans* was changing rapidly. The Vieux Carré has a certain Spanish-Caribbean feel because, just after the Cajuns arrived, a great fire swept through *Nouvelle Orleans*. In 1788 the old French buildings, made of aged cypress wood, were perfect fuel for a fire.

One of the oldest buildings in Quebec City, Canada, is another Ursuline Convent.

And when fire broke out, almost the entire Vieux Carré burned down. One of the few buildings left from the earlier time of the French is the Ursuline Convent. Since 1794, when a second great fire took place, much of the city was rebuilt in a mix of Spanish, French, and American styles. Beautiful wrought-iron balconies, ornamental gates, and Spanish courtyards adorned the city's reconstructed buildings. New Spanish fire codes requiring brick construction and slate roofs were a major reason the Vieux Carré escaped further destruction. Thus, today the famed French Quarter reflects architectural influences from other Spanish capitals such as Havana, Cuba.

The Spanish introduced more than architectural changes to *La Louisiane.* They introduced a new cuisine that included Louisiana's famous Shrimp Creole and spiced up our Jambalaya with Caribbean flavors. Other new foods included exotic fruits like plantains for breakfast and bananas for desserts. The Spanish language also influenced Louisiana with words like *Cabildo* and *lagniappe*, and, as we have seen, *New Iberia* — Iberia being the ancient name for the peninsula shared by Portugal and Spain.

As one travels down the Mississippi from Baton Rouge, Louisiana's civil parishes of Ascension, St. James, St. John, St. Charles, and then St. Bernard, reflect the way the Spanish organized their colonial churches. New Orleans residents are reminded every day of Spain's colonial rule as several city streets are named after Spanish governors such as Gálvez, Miró, and Carondelet. But even with these strong Iberian influences, French remained the dominant language of the colony throughout the Spanish era.

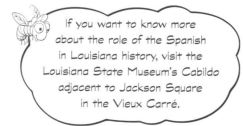

If you want to know more about the role of the Spanish in Louisiana history, visit the Louisiana State Museum's Cabildo adjacent to Jackson Square in the Vieux Carré.

FORTUNATELY FOR US, SPANISH COLONIALS ADDED A CERTAIN "SAUCE PIQUANTE" TO THE FIRE OF OUR CULTURAL GUMBO.

Beginning
of the
American
Era

N'Oncle Yvest,
Tell us about the Pirates!
Tell us about the Creoles!
Tell us about Andrew Jackson!

Mes chères,
Let me tell you
all about it . . .

Americans Take Control . . .

Even though the Spanish were busy seeking settlers from outside *La Louisiane*, they were not expecting the large number of English speakers who pressed into the colony from the new United States. The Cajuns and other French speakers of Spanish *La Louisiane* considered these Anglo folks from the continental interior as outsiders and in those days, referred to these English-speaking people as *Américains*.

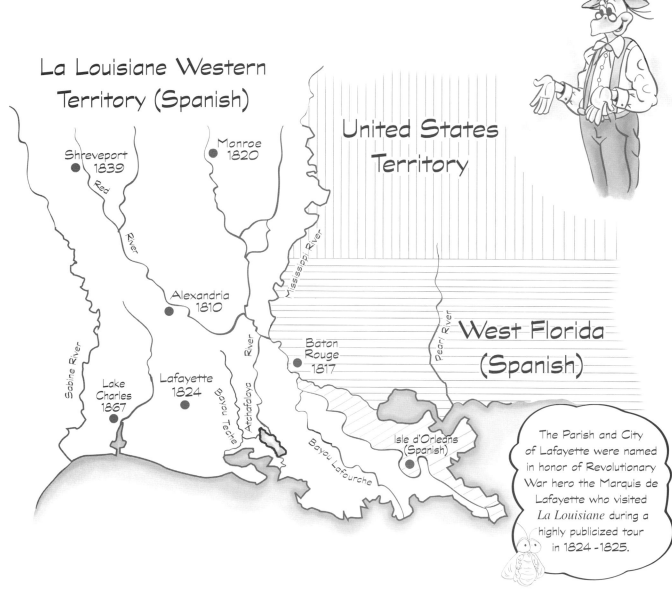

La Louisiane Western Territory (Spanish)

Shreveport 1839

Monroe 1820

Red River

Sabine River

Alexandria 1810

United States Territory

Mississippi River

Pearl River

West Florida (Spanish)

Bayou Teche

Atchafalaya River

Lake Charles 1867

Lafayette 1824

Baton Rouge 1817

Bayou Lafourche

Isle d'Orléans (Spanish)

The Parish and City of Lafayette were named in honor of Revolutionary War hero the Marquis de Lafayette who visited *La Louisiane* during a highly publicized tour in 1824 -1825.

By 1800 the *Américains*, who traveled down river from places such as Ohio, Tennessee, and Kentucky, soon dominated commerce in the Mississippi Valley. After the last Acadians arrived, vast expanses of *La Louisiane* were still unsettled and rapidly became populated by the *Américains*. These industrious Anglo-Americans, many of Scotch-Irish ancestry, created new settlements that would later become the modern day Crossroads of Alexandria and Deridder, the Red River's Shreveport and Bossier City, Monroe on the Ouachita River along with Minden, Ruston, and Bastrop, all centered in what is known today as Louisiana's Sportman's Paradise.

While Spanish-controlled *La Louisiane* attracted law-abiding citizens like the Acadians, Allemands, Isleños, and *Américains*, the colony's wetlands and marshes also attracted a wilder sort. Indeed, the Barataria region of *La Louisiane* with its countless waterways was ideal for pirates and soon became infamous for smuggling, contraband, and tales of buried loot. *La Louisiane's* most famous Baratarian was the mysterious Frenchman, Jean Lafitte. And in spite of their outlaw status, Lafitte's Baratarians would contribute greatly to the Americanization of *La Louisiane*. Today, the name of the region's National Park and Preserve commemorates Louisiana's fabled buccaneering past.

JEAN LAFITTE NATIONAL HISTORICAL PARK AND PRESERVE SITES

EUNICE
Prairie Culture, Dance and Music

LAFAYETTE
Acadian Culture

THIBODAUX
Wetlands Culture

BARATARIA PRESERVE

FRENCH QUARTER

CHALMETTE BATTLEFIELD

Scattered throughout Louisiana, like hidden pirate treasure, are visitor centers dedicated to interpreting the history and distinctive folk life of the state. Together these centers are known as the Jean Lafitte National Historical Park and Preserve.

In the Vieux Carré, the Spanish, French, and West Africans blended together over the years. To residents of the city, the product of this cultural blending became known as *Creole*. In Southwest Louisiana, however, the term *Creole* refers to the language and heritage of the region's French-speaking African Americans.

FOR YEARS THE VARIOUS INGREDIENTS OF *La Louisiane* GUMBEAUX SIMMERED UNDER THE SPANISH CROWN.

AS A RESULT OF THIS BLENDING, THE CULTURE OF *Nouvelle Orleans* BECAME CREOLE.

Creole IS A WORD THAT TODAY DESCRIBES ANYTHING TYPICAL OF THE REGION.

HERE YOU CAN FIND CREOLE TOMATOES, CREOLE OKRA AND EGGPLANT, ALL GROWN LOCALLY.

The Louisiana Purchase . . .

In 1803 during Thomas Jefferson's presidency, Spain's French-speaking colonists were surprised once again when it was announced that *La Louisiane* had been transferred back to France. After only twenty days, France, under the rule of Napoleon Bonaparte, sold *La Louisiane* to the United States for fifteen million dollars. Known today as the Louisiana Purchase, this act made Louisiana, as the *Américains* called the colony, a territory of the new United States.

The Louisiana Purchase — 1803

Louisiana Becomes 18th State — 1812

Louisiana's State Motto:
Union, Justice, Confidence.

After the American flag rose over the Place d'Armes on December 20, 1803, rapid changes took place in Louisiana. The name of *Nouvelle Orleans* was Americanized, of course, to New Orleans, and street signs were changed — again. The Spanish Calle Real, or the French Rue Royale, became Royal Street. The Louisiana Purchase more than doubled the size of the United States and unleashed the ingenuity and economic energy of the citizens of America's new territory. However, Louisiana's eight Florida parishes (those east of the Mississippi River) such as St. Tammany and Tangipahoa, would not become part of the territory until their inhabitants rebelled against Spain in 1810. Then in 1812, the vital importance of Louisiana was recognized. In that year Louisiana became the 18th state to join the United States.

After the Louisiana Purchase, the region prospered through hard work and determination. But there were ominous war clouds on Louisiana's horizon. During the Presidency of James Madison, America was again at war with England, and in 1814, the American capital of Washington was attacked and burned. New Orleans was the next British target — the city could just feel it. Like an approaching hurricane, the British were on the move, gathering an invasion force off Jamaica. However, American General Andrew Jackson was moving even faster toward New Orleans. When he and his experienced troops arrived, he took command of the city's defenses. Jackson then sent orders throughout the territory and rallied a rag-tag group of American Regulars, Acadians, Allemands, Creoles, West Africans, Isleños, Baratarians, and Native Americans on the sugar cane fields of the Chalmette Plantation just below the city.

The Baratarians were led by the legendary pirate Jean Lafitte, who assisted Jackson during the defense of New Orleans. Baratarians are said to have guided Jackson's troops through Louisiana's wetlands while buccaneers like Dominique Youx manned the American artillery.

By the morning of January 8, 1815, the Americans had dug in to await the British army. At dawn, the British, under General Sir Edward Packenham, advanced on Jackson's line. Bagpipes were blaring, and British Congreve rockets lit the fog-filled air. This English demonstration of power was awesome, yet the Americans did not flinch. Maybe it was the spices from the campfire gumbos, but there was definitely fire in their eyes. Within a few hours, the Americans soundly defeated the invading force of British Redcoats and tweeded Scots.

After the battle, the news of America's overwhelming victory over the British at Chalmette was electrifying. The British defeat became known in American newspapers as the Battle of New Orleans. The triumph freed Louisiana and all America from future threats of military invasion and unleashed the economic energy of its colorful citizens.

Learn how a peace treaty signed at Ghênt, Belgium, just two weeks before the battle, might have averted British losses at the Chalmette Battlefield — The battlefield is part of the Jean Lafitte National Historical Park and Preserve.

And the Story Continues . . .

N'ONCLE YVEST: So, *mes amis*, whether your roots are French, Spanish, West African, Allemand, Acadian, Creole, Isleño, Baratarian, Native American, Italian, Scottish, Irish, Américain, or anything else, all of us *Cajun Comiques* consider each of you an essential ingredient in Louisiana's distinctive multicultural heritage.

GUMBEAUX KIDS: *Merci beaucoup*, N'Oncle Yvest!

N'ONCLE YVEST: Any time, *mes chères. Bon chance*! And always remember —
Our Heritage Is Our Inheritance. I think you will have a lot to show your class tomorrow if you let that cultural gumbo simmer overnight!

GUMBEAUX KIDS: We sure will, N'Oncle Yvest. Mademoiselle Minou is going to be surprised by what we've put together! We are off to finish our class project — but not before we have just one taste of that delicious gumbo you've been cooking all afternoon. Let's eat!

*C'est tout . . .
That's all!*

Cajun
Comiques
Historic
Louisiana
Appendices

WANT TO LEARN MORE?

ON THE FOLLOWING PAGES,
YOU WILL FIND AN
INDEX, CHRONOLOGY,
GLOSSARY, BIBLIOGRAPHY,
VIRTUAL FIELD TRIPS,
AND AUTHORS' NOTES.

ALL THESE ARE
PROVIDED TO ASSIST
YOU IN FURTHER
UNDERSTANDING THE
UNIQUENESS OF
HISTORIC LOUISIANA.

Index

To assist you, words in the storyline, illustrations, and in the *Les Petits Comiques* notes are all indexed.

45

Index of Dates

Chronology

1682 – Major European powers vie for control of the New World.

1684 – La Salle leads an expedition to establish a colony in *La Louisiane*.

1698 – France renews its interest in colonization, sending Iberville to *La Louisiane*.

1699 – In January, Iberville and his crew sail into the Gulf of Mexico.

1706 – Bienville receives the news of his brother Iberville's death.

1713 – France hands over all of Acadia to the British in Treaty of Utrecht.

1715 – Natchitoches is founded by French Canadian officer Louis de Saint-Denis.

1718 – New Orleans is selected by Bienville as a permanent settlement site.

1719 – First West African slaves arrive in *La Louisiane* from Senegal.

1719 – Under John Law, German farmers settle in *La Louisiane*.

1743 – Bienville leaves New Orleans for France, never to return.

1755 – Acadians are deported from Nova Scotia.

1762 – France cedes *La Louisiane* to Spain at Fountainbleu.

1763 – In Canada, England defeats France to gain control of North America.

1766 – Colonists learn that France ceded its colony of *La Louisiane* to its ally Spain.

1768 – First wave of settlement by French-speaking Acadians completed.

1769 – General Alejandro O'Reilly secures Spanish control of their *La Luisiane*.

1776 – Spanish government aids Americans in the War of Independence.

1778 – Spanish Isleños from the Canary Islands begin settling *La Louisiane*.

1779 – *La Louisiane's* Acadian and German militia battle the British.

1785 – Second wave of French-speaking Acadians arrive in *La Louisiane*.

1788 – Devastating fire destroys much of old French New Orleans.

1794 – Second fire damages New Orleans once again.

1800 – *Américains* start to settle in *La Louisiane*.

1803 – United States completes the Louisiana Purchase during Thomas Jefferson's presidency.

1810 – Louisiana's Florida parishes secured from Spain.

1812 – Louisiana becomes the 18th State of the Union, and War of 1812 begins.

1814 – Washington, DC attacked and burned by the British.

1815 – American victory and British defeat at the Battle of New Orleans.

1847 – The American Henry Wadsworth Longfellow's poem *Evangeline* is published.

1995 – La Salle's ship *La Belle* discovered in Matagorda Bay, Texas.

Glossary

A

Acadia: The Cajuns' original paradise in the wilds of Canada; now present day Nova Scotia.

Alexandria: City in the Crossroads of Louisiana nestled on the banks of the Red River.

Allemand: Cajun French term for a *German* as in the town of Des Allemands.

Américains: French term for Anglo-Americans who spoke English only.

Appalachians: Mountains that were originally the eastern border of *La Louisiane*.

Atchafalaya: Native American name of a river flowing from the Mississippi to the Gulf of Mexico.

Attakapas: Native American tribe for whom the *Poste des Attakapas* was named.

Avoyelles: A civil parish in Louisiana named after its original Native American inhabitants.

B

Baratarians: Followers of Jean Lafitte who hid in the Barataria wetlands of South Louisiana.

Baton Rouge: French term for *Red Stick;* spot where Iberville sighted the Istrouma poles.

Bayougoula: Native tribe in colonial times; today a town, Bayou Goula, on the River Road.

Belle: *La Belle*, name of La Salle's ship on his ill-fated return expedition to Louisiana.

Bienville: Jean Baptiste le Moyne, Sieur de Bienville, Canadian born; first governor of Louisiana.

Biloxi: City in Mississippi named after the Biloxi Indians; location of Iberville's first fortification.

Bon Papa: Lead of seven ships chartered by Spain to carry Acadians to Louisiana in 1785.

Bonaparte: Napoleon Bonaparte ruled France and sold Louisiana to the United States.

Bonjour, mes infants: Cajun French for *Greetings my little ones.*

Borgne: Name means *one-eyed;* Lake Borgne is only half a lake as French sailors saw it.

Bouligny: Francisco Bouligny, Spanish officer under Gálvez who founded the city of New Iberia.

Brest: Seaport in France from which Iberville's expedition set sail across the Atlantic for Louisiana.

C

Cabildo: Seat of the Spanish colonial government in the Vieux Carré; now the Louisiana State Museum.

Caddo: A civil parish in Louisiana named after its original Native American inhabitants.

Canada: Birthplace of Iberville and Bienville and other early Louisiana settlers.

Canary Islands: The homeland of Louisiana's Isleños located off the coast of Spain.

Cajuns: A variation of *Les Acadians*, Louisiana's French-speaking settlers from Canada's Acadia.

Calle: Spanish word for a city street, for example, *Calle Real* is Royal Street.

Carlos III: King of Spain when France ceded *La Louisiane* to the Spanish at Fountainbleu.

Carondelet: Spanish governor of Louisiana following Gálvez and Miró.

Carré: French term for a city square or rectangle, as in the *Vieux Carré*.

Chalmette: Suburb of New Orleans and site of the Battle of New Orleans on January 8, 1815.

Chien: French word for *dog or hound*.

Chitamacha: Oldest of the four sovereign Native American tribes of Louisiana at Charenton.

Cité Croissant: French for the *Crescent City;* nickname for New Orleans.

Civil Parishes: In Louisiana, the political equivalent of a county in other states.

Comique: Cajun French term meaning *comical or funny.*

Compagnies Détachées: French for *detached companies*, basic colonial military organization.

Congo Square: One source of West African rhythms in Louisiana music; today's Armstrong Park.

Côte des Allemands: The German Coast of colonial *La Louisiane* on the Mississippi.

Coureur de Bois: French for *runner of the woods* — a French Canadian frontiersman.

Coushatta: Sovereign Native American tribe of Louisiana; town between Shreveport and Natchitoches.

Creole: Today it means people and things, especially certain foods, unique to Louisiana.

Cuba: Island where Havana, the former capital of the Spanish New World, is located.

Decima: Spanish ballad sung by the Isleños, a form of musical poetry that tells a story.

Duc d'Orleans: The Duke of Orleans, after whom New Orleans was named by Bienville.

England: One of the European colonial powers that fought for control of North America.

Eunice: City in Louisiana's Acadia Parish where the Prairie Acadian Cultural Center is located.

Evangeline: The heroine of Longfellow's narrative poem about the Acadian's *Grand Derangement.*

Filé: Ground sassafras leaves used by Native Americans and others to thicken gumbo.

Florida: The Spanish territory from which eight Louisiana civil parishes were formed.

France: One of the European colonial powers that fought for control of North America.

French and Indian War: Resulted in the French forfeiting all of New France to England.

Fountainbleu: Palace in France where in 1762 the French gave their colony of *La Louisiane* to Spain.

G

Gálvez: Spanish governor of Louisiana who fought the British during the American Revolutionary War.

***Grand Derangement*:** The years of wandering after the Acadians were exiled from Nova Scotia.

***Grandpère*:** Cajun French word for one's *Grandfather*.

Gumbeaux: The Cajun Comiques way of describing the unique multicultural heritage of Louisiana.

Gumbo: Roux-based stew-like dish considered standard dinner fare throughout Louisiana.

H

Havana: City in Cuba, largest island in the Caribbean and former capital of Spain's New World government.

Heritage: Unique cultural gifts from our past that enrich our daily lives.

Houma: A quaint city in Southeast Louisiana named after the Houma Native American Indian tribe.

I

Iberville: Pierre le Moyne, Sieur d'Iberville, Canadian naval officer and Bienville's older brother.

***Isle d'Orleans*:** The east bank of the Mississippi south of Baton Rouge down to the river's mouth.

Isleños: Term for early Louisiana settlers from the Canary Islands off the coast of Spain.

Istrouma: Poles that once marked the tribal boundaries between the Bayougoula and Houma Indians.

J

Jackson: Andrew Jackson, hero of the Battle of New Orleans, President of the United States.

Jambalaya: A special sauce piquante and rice-based dish eaten with gusto throughout Louisiana.

Jazz: A distinctive music style generally associated with the city of New Orleans.

Jefferson: Thomas Jefferson, President of the United States during the Louisiana Purchase.

Jena Band of Choctaw: A sovereign tribe of Louisiana living around the town of Jena.

L

La Salle: Robert de La Salle, explorer who claimed the entire Mississippi river valley for France.

Lafayette: Marquis de Lafayette, French military hero of the American Revolution.

Lafayette: City known for its Cajun heritage and site of the Acadian Cultural Center.

Lafitte: Jean Lafitte, mysterious buccaneer who assisted Jackson in defending Louisiana.

Lafourche: A bayou that branches out from the Mississippi and flows to the Gulf of Mexico.

Lagniappe: A word of Spanish origin that in Louisiana means to add a little something extra.

Law: John Law, clever Scottish businessman who convinced German farmers to settle in *La Louisiane*.

Longfellow: Henry Wadsworth Longfellow immortalized the Acadians in his poem, *Evangeline*.

Louis XIV: King Louis the 14th, *The Sun King* who ruled when La Salle claimed *La Louisiane* for France.

Louis XV: King Louis the 15th, French king who ceded *La Louisiane* to Spain at palace of Fountainbleu.

Louisiana: America's name for the 18th state, admitted into the Union in 1812.

Louisiana Purchase: In 1803 the acquisition by the United States of France's *La Louisiane*.

Louisiane: *La Louisiane*, the French colonial name for the Louisiana territory.

Luisiane: *La Luisiane*, the Spanish colonial name for the Louisiana territory.

M

Mademoiselle: French for a *young or unmarried woman*.

Madison: James Madison, American President during the War of 1812.

Mais, ecoute dont ça: Cajun French for *Listen to that*.

Málaga: Town in southern Spain which many settlers of colonial New Iberia were from.

Maurepas: Lake named after Pontchartrain's son, who was also a prominent minister of France.

Mémere: Cajun French word for one's *Grandmother*.

Merci beaucoup: French for *Thank you very much*.

Mes amis: Cajun French for *My friends*.

Mes chères: Cajun French for *My dears*.

Minou: Cajun French, an endearing name for any cat.

Miró: Spanish governor of Louisiana who helped settle the Isleños and Cajuns.

Mississippi: The great river Native Americans called the *Father of Waters*.

Mobile: City in Alabama named after the Mobile Indians and site of Iberville's second fortification.

Monroe: City in Northeast Louisiana in colonial times named *Poste des Ouachita*.

Montreal: Canadian city from which La Salle and Tonti started their journey of Louisiana discovery.

Multicultural: Of or pertaining to cooperation amongst people of different origins.

N

N'Oncle: Cajun French for *Uncle*, or a simple term of endearment for an older male family member.

Natchitoches: Native American tribe; oldest town in the Louisiana Purchase founded in 1715.

Native American: The indigenous bands of people who originally inhabited all of *La Louisiane*.

Nénaine: Cajun French word for one's *Godmother*.

New France: Northern areas of the American continent originally controlled by the French.

New Iberia: City on Bayou Teche during colonial era named Nuevo Iberia.

Nouvelle Acadie: The Cajun French name for the Cajuns' *New Acadia* in Louisiana.

Nouvelle Orleans: The city of New Orleans named after France's *Duc d'Orleans*.

Nova Scotia: Province in present day Canada originally settled by French Acadians.

O

Okra: Popular West African vegetable, the name of which was given to the dish in which it is used.

Opelousas: City in colonial times named the Poste des Opelousas after Native American tribe.

Ouachita: Native American tribe, name of a river and a civil parish in Louisiana.

O'Reilly: General Alejandro O'Reilly, military governor sent by Spain to *La Louisiane*.

P

Packenham: General Sir Edward Packenham, British commander killed at Chalmette.

Parrain: Cajun French word for one's *Godfather*.

Place d'Armes: A drill field for French soldiers laid out like Jackson Square in New Orleans.

Plaquemines: A civil parish in Louisiana which means *persimmons* in a Native American tongue.

Ponchatoula: Louisiana's strawberry capital whose name is of Native American origin.

Pontchartrain: Comte de Pontchartrain, Louis XIV's minister who authorized Iberville's voyage.

Q

Quebec: Canadian city in which the Ursuline Convent is also one of its oldest buildings.

Quelle bonheur: Cajun French for *What luck*.

R

Red River: A meandering red tinted river flowing through the cities of Shreveport and Alexandria.

Red Beans and Rice: Traditional New Orleans meal served on Mondays – wash day.

Rigolets: Passage from Lakes Borgne to Pontchartrain, French for *a channel of water*.

Rocky Mountains: Mountain range that defined the western border of La Salle's *La Louisiane*.

Roux: Starting ingredient of any gumbo; flour darkly browned with cooking oil in a kettle or pot.

Rue: French for *a city street*, for example, *Rue Bourbon* was Bourbon Street.

S

Sauce Piquante: A spicy tomato-based sauce used in a number of flavorful Louisiana dishes.

Senegal: The modern day country from which most Louisiana slaves were transported.

Shreveport: City in northwest corner of Louisiana located on the banks of the Red River.

Shrimp Creole: A tangy Louisiana shrimp and rice dish with a decided Caribbean flavor.

Spain: One of the European colonial powers that vied for control of North America.

St. Jean: Body of water flowing into Lake Pontchartrain, known today as Bayou St. John.

St. Louis: French Catholic saint who was also King Louis IX (9th) of France.

Sun King: A title for King Louis XIV (14th) when the territory of *La Louisiane* was claimed by La Salle.

Tangipahoa: A civil parish in Louisiana named after a Native American tribe.

Tchefuncte: A river in Louisiana with a name of Native American origin.

Tchoupitoulas: In colonial times a Native American tribe that lived near New Orleans.

Teche: A bayou that flows through the prairies of southwest Louisiana into the Atchafalaya River.

***Terre-aux-Boeufs*:** French for *Land of the Wild Oxen*, present day St Bernard Parish.

Thibodaux: Historic city on Bayou Lafourche and Wetlands Acadian Cultural Center location.

Ti: Contraction of the Cajun French petit meaning *little or small*.

Tonti: Henri di Tonti, La Salle's fellow explorer who was of Italian ancestry.

Treaty of Paris: Agreement of 1763 whereby England took control of New France.

***Tres malheureux*:** Cajun French for *Very sad.*

Tunica-Biloxi: Tribe of Louisiana after which the town of Tunica is named.

Ursuline: An order of Catholic nuns, whose convent is one of the oldest buildings in the Vieux Carré.

Utrecht: Treaty of 1713 by which all of French Acadia was handed over to the English.

Versailles: Court of the King of France near Paris, and name of a former plantation in Louisiana.

Vieux Carré: French for *Old Square*, synonymous with the New Orleans French Quarter.

War of Independence: War during which Spanish Governor Gálvez provided military assistance.

West Africa: Region of the world from which slaves were transported to Louisiana.

Youx: Dominique Youx, Baratarian made famous by the Battle of New Orleans.

Zydeco: A distinctive music style generally associated with the Louisiana countryside.

Bibliography

Blume, Helmut. *The German Coast During the Colonial Era 1722–1803.* Translated by Ellen C. Merrill. The German-Acadian Coast Historical and Genealogical Society. Destrehan, LA. 1990.

Brasseaux, Carl A. *France's Forgotten Legion.* Louisiana State University Press. Baton Rouge, LA. 2000.

Brasseaux, Carl A. *The Founding of New Acadia — The Beginnings of Acadian Life in Louisiana 1765–1803.* Louisiana State University Press. Baton Rouge, LA. 1987.

Caughey, John Walton. *Bernardo de Galvez in Louisiana 1776–1783.* Pelican Publishing Company. Gretna, LA. 1991.

Conrad, Glenn R.(Editor). *The French Experience in Louisiana.* Center for Louisiana Studies, University of Southwestern Louisiana, Lafayette, LA. 1995.

Cummins, Light Townsend. *Spanish Observes and the American Revolution 1775–1783.* Louisiana State University Press. Baton Rouge, LA. 1991.

Daigle, Jules O. (Rev. Msgr.). *A Dictionary of the Cajun Language.* Edward Brothers, Inc. Ann Arbor, MI. 1984.

Davis, Edwin Adams. *Louisiana — The Pelican State.* Louisiana State University Press. Baton Rouge, LA. 1959.

Din, Gilbert C. *The Canary Islanders.* Louisiana State University Press. Baton Rouge, LA. 1988.

Din, Gilbert C. *Francisco Bouligny — A Bourbon Soldier in Spanish Louisiana.* Louisiana State University Press. Baton Rouge, LA. 1993.

Gayerré, Charles. *History of Louisiane, IV Volumes.* Claitor's Publishing. Baton Rouge, LA. Louisiana Classic Series Reprint 1974.

Giraud, Marcel. *A History of French Louisiana, V Volumes.* Translated by Joseph C. Lambert. Louisiana State University Press. 1990.

Hall, Gwendolyn Midlo. *Africans in Colonial Louisiana.* Louisiana State University Press. Baton Rouge, LA. 1992.

Fortier, Alcée. *A History of Louisiana, IV Volumes.* Claitor's Publishing. Baton Rouge, LA. Reprinted 1966.

Richard, Carl J. *The Louisiana Purchase — Louisiana Life Series No. 7.* The Center for Louisiana Studies. Lafayette, LA. 1995.

Ruston, William Faulkner. *The Cajun: From Acadia to Louisiana.* Farrar Straus Giroux. New York, NY. 1979.

State of Louisiana. *Official Highway Map.* Department of Transportation and Development. Baton Rouge, LA. 2002.

Virtual Field Trips

Check out the following Web sites for additional resources directly related to *Cajun Comiques Historic Louisiana*. These sites provide kids of all ages with information about fun-oriented multicultural experiences throughout the state.

EACH VIRTUAL FIELD TRIP STARTS WITH A WEB LINK ON THIS PAGE. EXPLORE EACH SITE TO LOCATE THE RESOURCES YOU SEEK.

Experiences in the Greater New Orleans Area

NPS French Quarter Visitor Center, New Orleans – www.nps.gov/jela/pphtm/facilities.html
Cabildo - Louisiana State Museum, New Orleans – lsm.crt.state.la.us [See Properties]
NPS Chalmette Battlefield, Chalmette – www.nps.gov/jela/pphtm/facilities.html
Los Isleños Heritage and Cultural Center, St. Bernard – www.losislenos.org
NPS Barataria Preserve, Marrero – www.nps.gov/jela/pphtm/facilities.html
Old U. S. Mint - Louisiana State Museum, New Orleans – lsm.crt.state.la.us [See Properties]
New Orleans African American Museum, New Orleans – www.noaam.org

Experiences in Louisiana's Bayou Country

NPS Wetlands Acadian Cultural Center, Thibodaux – www.nps.gov/jela/pphtm/facilities.html
Laurel Valley Village Store Museum, Thibodaux – www.lafourche-tourism.org/welcome.htm [See Attractions]
Rural Life Museum, Baton Rouge – rurallife.lsu.edu
Chitimacha Cultural Center, Charenton – www.chitimacha,gov
Longfellow-Evangeline State Historic Site, St. Martinville – www.crt.state.la.us/crt/parks [See Historic Sites]
The African American Museum, St. Martinville – www.stmartinparish-la.org/tourism_attractions.htm
German-Acadian Coast Historical and Genealogical Society – www.gachgs.com

Experiences in Louisiana's Prairie Country

NPS Acadian Cultural Center, Lafayette – www.nps.gov/jela/pphtm/facilities.html
Vermilionville Living History Museum and Village, Lafayette – www.vermilionville.org
Acadian Village, Lafayette – www.acadianvillage.org
NPS Prairie Acadian Cultural Center, Eunice – www.nps.gov/jela/pphtm/facilities.html
Coushatta Reservation, Elton – www.coushattatribela.org

Experiences Along Louisiana's Red River

Fort Jean Baptiste State Historic Park, Natchitoches – www.crt.state.la.us/crt/parks [See Historic Sites]
Los Adaes State Historic Park, Robeline – www.crt.state.la.us/crt/parks [See Historic Sites]
Old Courthouse Museum, Natchitoches – lsm.crt.state.la.us [See Properties]

Experiences in Avoyelles and Beyond

Biloxi-Tunica Tribe, Marksville – www.tunica.org
Marksville State Historic Site, Marksville – www.crt.state.la.us/crt/parks [See Historic Sites]
Poverty Point State Historic Site, Epps – www.crt.state.la.us/crt/parks [See Historic Sites]

For Virtual Field Trip Updates

Web sites change often so we suggest checking in at: www.cajuncomiques.com *for up-to-date links.*

Authors' Notes

François Ferret — aka Wallace P. Faucheux — is the artistic force behind the *Cajun Comiques.* He is a native of the New Orleans area, growing up on the city's West Bank near the Jean Lafitte National Historic Park's Barataria Preserve. As a youngster, Wally spent his weekends and summers with family in Louisiana's Plantation Country. A noted New Orleans commercial artist, Wally has a talent for communicating with others the *joie de vivre* associated with historic Louisiana. Wally himself is part of the cultural gumbo of the Pelican State, being a direct descendant of both French and German settlers of the *Côte des Allemands.*

Toulouse Le Turtle — aka Guy N. Faucheux — is the historical research arm of the *Cajun Comiques.* Also a native of New Orleans, he grew up near the Jean Lafitte National Historic Park's Chalmette Battlefield. Guy was doubly blessed by growing up in the Crescent City and by being able to spend lots of time with his extended Acadian family in Thibodaux, the site of the Park Service's Wetlands Acadian Cultural Center. Like Wally, Guy has a calling to communicate to others the uniqueness of *La Louisiane Historique.* He cherishes Louisiana's values and encourages everyone to appreciate that "Our Heritage Is Our Inheritance."

La Famille Faucheux

The Faucheux family name arrived in La Louisiane in 1728 when a young soldier from France, François Faucheux, disembarked in the colony as a member of a *compagnie détachée.* From those colonial times, the Faucheux family has grown and flourished in the State. The Faucheux family name has participated in Louisiana's major historical events including fighting under the command of the Spanish Governor Gálvez in the American Revolutionary War, under the command of General Andrew Jackson during the Battle of New Orleans, and during the Civil War as members of the Army of Northern Virginia. In that same tradition, many other Faucheux family members have served in our country's armed forces in modern times — some making the ultimate sacrifice.

Wally and Guy are "technically" unrelated and are actually members of two divergent lines of Louisiana's Faucheux family. Wally married Guy's sister, Aimée Faucheux, who is La Famille Faucheux's publishing and print production specialist. Aimée's birthday is on the anniversary of the Louisiana Purchase. Guy is married to Deanne Faucheux, née, Deanne Mary Rowan. They were married, appropriately, on the anniversary date of the Battle of New Orleans. Their daughter, Jeanne Faucheux, and Deanne combined their professional skills to advance this publication as the family's editorial staff.

SPECIAL THANKS TO PEGGY LAVIGNE FAUCHEUX
OF NEW ORLEANS FOR HER LOVE OF LOUISIANA HISTORY
AND TO NORMAN P. FAUCHEUX OF THIBODAUX FOR HIS INSIGHT
INTO THE SUBTLETIES OF THE CAJUN-FRENCH LANGUAGE.